Star Wars Character

Description Guide

The Ultimate Encyclopedia of Star

Wars Characters, Creatures, and

Villains

Luke Williams

Table of Contents:

A New Hope

Note: *The Galactic Standard Calendar was the standard measurement of time in the Star Wars Universe, centering the Coruscan cycle, which has 368 days --- with each day lasting 24 standard hours. The Battle of Yavin is used as a standard measuring point, with BBY standing for Before Battle of Yavin and ABY standing for After Battle of Yavin.*

1. Admiral Conan Antonio Motti (Born N/A - Died 0 BBY)

As one of the highest-ranking Imperial officers, Admiral Conan Antonio Motti was very confident in the Empire and in the invincibility of the Death Star. Only Grand Moff Wilhuff Tarkin outranked him on the battle station, but he didn't believe in the powers of the Force, prompting him to even taunt Darth Vader when Vader failed to find the whereabouts of the rebels who stole the plans for the Death Star. This led to Vader saying "I find your lack of faith disturbing", where he ended up getting choked by Darth Vader without Vader even touching him.

2. Biggs Darklighter (born N/A - Died during Battle of Yavin)

A human starpilot who fought for the Alliance To Restore The Republic, Biggs grew up in the desert world of Tattoine and was a close friend to Luke Skywalker. He was one of the rebels who pioneered the plan to steal the blueprint of the Death Star, which led to Luke Skywalker ultimately destroying the Empire's superweapon. However, Biggs was killed by Darth Vader before Luke was able to save him.

3. Luke Skywalker (Born 19 BBY - Died N/A)

A Force-sensitive Human male who was the main protagonist in the Star Wars: A New Hope, Luke Skywalker was the son of Anakin Skywalker and Padme Amidala. He was led to believe that he was just another normal human being, until he came and crossed paths with R2-D2 and C3PO, droids who were carrying a secret message for Obi-Wan Kenobi. These droids were also former possessions of his father, Anakin Skywalker who turned into the fearsome Darth Vader --- further leading him onto a path where his destiny truly belonged. Luke led the rebels and its armies to many victories --- even destroying the Death Star with the help of others.

4. Leia Organa (Born 19 BBY - Died N/A)

Leia Organa was the twin sister of Luke Skywalker and one of the main characters in the Star Wars: A New Hope. Unlike his twin brother Luke who was raised in a normal household, Leia was raised in a royal family after her mother died upon childbirth. Like her mother before her, she used her political and royal stronghold in order to secure the peace, culture and livelihood of her own people. During the Galactic Civil War, Leia was entrusted the blueprint of the Death Star, which the rebels stole in order to destroy the Empire's super weapon. This event led her to Obi-Wan Kenobi, one of the last Jedi Masters still in hiding, and her biological brother Luke Skywalker. Together, they acted and became part of so many events that ultimately led to the restoration of the Republic

5. BoShek

Boshek was a male force-sensitive Corellian smuggler who had imminent skills and talent for piloting. He was really enthusiastic about learning the Force, but had little to no success in it until Obi-Wan Kenobi advised him to get away from his shady lifestyle and "embrace the light" in order to fully unlock his potential to use the Force. Taking it to heart, he tried to live an honest life while meditating to the Force, but his tenuous sensitivity to the Force led to no avail. Still, his piloting skills are to be commended.

6. Boba Fett

Boba Fett was a male bounty hunter. His late father, Jango Fett, was one of the strongest bounty hunters during his time and was even used as a genetic blueprint for the clone warriors that the Republic commissioned to be made to supplement their army. As a young boy, he was present when his father was killed and beheaded by Master Windu after his father tried to escape the Jedi inquiry. This event gave him a grudge and thirst for revenge against the Jedi that remained even after he grew into adulthood.

7. Dr. Cornelius Evazan (Born N/A - Died 0 BBY)

A human male from the planet of Alsakan, Cornelius Evazan was once a very talented and promising cosmetic surgeon, until he decided to play with his subjects and practice experimental cosmetic surgery --- often leaving his patients horrible disfigured. His face was almost cut in two and was horribly disfigured after he was hunted down by a bounty hunter who learned about his gruesome experimental surgeries. He was killed by Jedi Master Obi-Wan Kenobi

8. Jon "Dutch" Vander (Born 34 BBy - Died 0 BBY)

Trained as a fighter pilot in the Imperial Academy, Jon "Dutch" Vander was a human senior pilot who went from Imperial starpilot into a rebel pilot after learning of the Empire's true nature. He joined the Rebel Alliance after he was instructed to bomb his own home planet --- something that he cannot and will never do. During the Battle of Yavin, he was shut down by Darth Vader while piloting his aircraft.

9. Figrin D'an

Figrin D'an was a male Bith who played the "kloo horn" as a musician. He was the frontman for the music band known as the Modal Nodes and he was present during the incident where Jedi-in-hiding Obi-Wan Kenobi slashed of the arm of Ponda Baba in defense of Luke Skywalker. His band played in a pub in the Mos Eisley spaceport in the planet of Tattoine.

10. Garven Dreis (Born N/A - Died 0 BBY)

Garven Dreis was a human Starpilot commander who commanded the Red Squadron in service of the Alliance to Restore The Republic. Although greatly skilled in piloting and in combat, he proved to be no match for the Sith Lord Darth Vader, who killed him during a skirmish.

11. General Jan Dodonna (born 65 BBY - Died 24 ABY)

General Jan Dodonna served both the Galactic Republic and Galactic Empire --- one of the few Generals to do so. Throughout his long years of experience both in service and in combat, General Dodonna was often considered a "legend" and an authority in modern space combat. He was often seen deducing strategies and tactics for battle, which often turned the tide of battle towards his faction's favor.

12. Greedo (Born N/A - Died 0 BBY)

A male rodian bounty hunter who grew up in the desert planet of Tatooine, he was hired by the Trade Federation to kidnap Chi Eekway and Che Amanwe Papanoida, the daughters of Chairman Papanoida. He was also hired by rich mercenaries such as Jabba the Hutt to do assassinations for him. He met his end when he tried to confront the smuggler Hans Solo, who proved to be too cunning, skillful and intelligent for him.

13. Han Solo

Han Solo was the captain of the spacecraft "The Millennium Falcon" and is also said to be the galaxy's most loved rogue. He seems to be a witty, cunning and crafty gambler who looks after no one else other than himself. However, as time went on, he proved that he possessed a caring heart and helped not only Obi-Wan Kenobi and Anakin but also Princess Leia in escaping the hands of the Empire. He played a vital role in the restoration of the Republic through his piloting skills and cunning escape strategies.

14. Jabba "The Hutt" Desilijic Tiure (Born 600 BBY - Died 4 ABY)

A notorious underground gang leader governing a large criminal organization under his wing, Jabba The Hutt was known throughout the galaxy. During his prime years, Jabba was known as one of the most notorious and powerful crime lords in the galaxy. It was said that he even had contact with Prince Xizor, the criminal head of the Black Sun Syndicate. His business extended from spice-smuggling, mercenary killing, gunrunning, slavery, and even outright piracy. He was killed by Luke's sister, Leia Organo.

15. Lak Sivrak (Born 8 BBY - Died 4 ABY)

As a male scout who worked for the Galactic Constabulary, Lak Sivrak became famous after he started working for the Galactic Empire. Although he worked for the Empire loyally, Sivrak was unaware of the evil and tyranny of his employers. After stumbling over a hidden settlement of members of the Alliance to Restore the Republic, he decided to help them. This started his defection from being an Empire loyalist to Republic supporter. He died while piloting his spacecraft in the Battle of Endor.

The Empire Strikes Back

Note: The Galactic Standard Calendar was the standard measurement of time in the Star Wars Universe, centering around the Coruscan solar cycle, which has 368 days --- with each day lasting 24 standard hours. The Battle of Yavin is used as a standard measuring point, with BBY standing for Before Battle of Yavin and ABY standing for After Battle of Yavin.

1. 4LOM

One of the most peculiar and interesting characters in the Star Wars Sage is 4LOM, a droid manufactured by Industrial Automation. Ambitious and cunning, a programming glitch allowed 4LOM to override his settings and become an independent LOM-series protocol droid. He started of as an intergalactic thief and then later turned into a cunning bounty hunter who rubbed elbows with other notorious space pirates such as Boba Fett.

2. Kendal Ozzel (Born N/A - Died 3 ABY)

Born into a wealthy family, Kendal Ozzel was a military officer who studied on several Core Military institutes in the galaxy. He was, however, delegated into a teaching position because his superiors thought that he lacked proper field training and experience. Still, he showed prowess and skill running the important missions for the Galactic Empire after the Republic was abolished, and he had a great relationship with Senator Palpatine. Darth Vader, however, was not impressed when Kendal Ozzel allowed some members of the Rebel Alliance to escape because of his tactical blunder --- and Darth Vader eventually killed him via telekinesis.

3. Firmus Piett (Born 39 BBY - Died 4 ABY)

The last admiral of the Death Squadron, Darth Vader's personal fleet that is under the wing of the Imperial Navy, Firmus Piett came from a humble background unlike most of his contemporaries. While serving as a constabulary in his him planet Axxila, he made quite a number of arrests and reprimanded a lot of smugglers and pirates, thereby gaining the attention of the Imperial Center. He died when a star ship piloted by Arvel Crynyd crashed on to the bridge of the imperial fleet's flagship, Executor, and rammed him to death.

4. Bossk

Affiliated with Boba Fett's syndicate, Bossk was a bounty hunter who was known throughout the galaxy as a "Wookie executioner". He was feared because of his cunning and the Jedi killed efficiency when it comes to killing wookies, and he even mentored the young Boba Fett right after his father Jango Fett, during the Clone Wars. He was also commissioned by Darth Vader to search and find Han Solo's ship, the Millennium Falcon.

5. Dak Ralter (Born 17 BBY - Died 2 ABY)

A human male starship pilot who possessed great flying skills that even rival that of top Imperial admirals, Dak Ralter served the Alliance to Restore the Republic when the Galactic Civil War erupted. He was a friend of the legendary Jedi Knight, Luke Skywalker, and served as Luke's personal gunner during the war. He died at his station during the Battle of Hoth, 30 months after the Battle of Yavin.

6. Dengar

A male Corellian bounty hunter who worked alongside other popular bounty hunters such as Boba Fett, Dengar was a cunning working known to have been in operation even before the days of the Clone War. He was part of the bounty hunter group commissioned by Darth Vader to capture Han Solo and his ship, the Millennium Falcon.

7. Maximilian Veers (Born 48 BBY - Died 10 ABY)

A male human Major General for the Imperial Army of the Galactic Empire, Maximilian Veers was known for his prowess and leadership in many important battles during the course of his military service. He graduated at the top of his class and gained momentum in the military ranks --- enough to get even the attention of Darth Vader and the Galactic Empire after defeating a group of Rebel Invasion Force. He was sent on a suicide mission by Executor Sedriss QL, who hated the fact that he served and survived Darth Vader after the Empire's defeat --- leading one of the greatest Empire tacticians and military heroes to his own death.

8. IG-88

Pretty much like the droid 4LOM, IG-88 was another rogue droid who overrode his controls and programming to become a bounty hunter. He was part of the bounty hunter group that was summoned and commissioned by the Sith Lord, Darth Vader, to track and hunt down Han Solo's ship, the Millennium Falcon. He also considered Boba Fett, his comrade and companion during their hunt for Han Solo, as his single and greatest bounty hunter rival.

9. Lando Calrissian (Born 30 BBY - Died N/A)

A human who shared Han Solo's traits such as smuggling, gambling, playing cards and even womanizing, Lando Calrissian became one of the most important generals of the Rebel Alliance who fought to usurp the power from the oppressive Empire. He was the original owner of the famous starship, the Millennium Falcon --- that is, before he lost it to fellow gambler and smuggler Han Solo. He piloted the Millennium Falcon to the core of the Death Star II and fired the shot that ultimately destroyed it, allowing the Rebel Alliance to win one of the most important battles in history.

10. Lobot

He was a human man who was handling most of the
battlefield and military calculations for the Galactic Empire.
Aided by his personal robot, AJ^6 Cyborg Construct, Lobot.
However, he soon began working alongside the smuggler
Lando Calrissian, who was also connected to the rebel Han
Solo. He was the Baron Adminstrator of Cloud City and as
the city's computer-liaison officer, the implants that he had
in him enabled him to communicate with the city's central
network.

The Phantom Menace

*Note: The Galactic Standard Calendar was the standard measurement of time in the Star Wars Universe, centering the Coruscan solar cycle, which has 368 days --- with each day lasting 24 standard hours. The Battle of Yavin is used as a standard measuring point, with **BBY** standing for Before Battle of Yavin and **ABY** standing for After Battle of Yavin.*

1. Qui Gon Jinn (Born 92 BBY – Died 32 BBY)

As a revered master Jedi with an unconventional yet powerful style, Qui Gon Jinn was considered as one of the strongest members of the Jedi Council. He was trained by Count Dooku before the count fell to the Dark Side, which explains why Qui-Gon is such as strong and intelligent character himself. Attuned strongly to the Force, he seems to have a "need" to help those who are weak and meek, often leading him on side missions that are outside his mission protocols. He is the master of Obi Wan Kenobi and for a short time he also mentored the young Anakin Skywalker. He was killed in his battle against Darth Maul.

2. Obi-Wan Kenobi (Born 57 BBY – Died 0 BBY)

Obi-Wan Kenobi, also known as Uncle Ben Kenobi during his exile (after the Jedi's defeat in the hands of the Empire) is considered as one of the most renowned Jedis in the history of Star Wars. Characterized by a calm demeanor that swiftly charms people, we has the complete opposite of his aggressive and outgoing student Anakin Skywalker. He is very skilled with the light saber and he is also one of the highest-ranking masters in the Jedi Council.

3. Queen Padmé Naberrie Amidala (Born 46 BBY – Died 26 BBY)

Queen Padmé Amidala came from the Planet of Naboo and served a vital role in liberating the people who were oppressed by the political powers in the Star Wars universe. She is the wife of Anakin Skywalker and the mother of Luke Skywalker and Princess Leia Organa Solo, three of the most important characters in the galaxy. Through her life, she fought for the freedom and liberation of the small folk and was respected even by her enemies because of her cunning, charm and political will.

4. Anakin Skywalker / Darth Vader (Born 42 BBY – Died 4 ABY)

A legendary Jedi in his own right, Anakin was born as a slave but was discovered by the Jedi Master Qui-Gon Jinn. Anakin was prophesized as the chosen one who would "balance the Force" and lead the Jedi to victory against the Sith. Anakin possessed the most potential in any Jedi, having a midi-chlorian count of 20,000 units per cell, the highest known number since the Jedi started this method of testing. A high number of midi-chlorians meant that a person or an entity will be much more sensitive to the Force, making him or her a great candidate to wield the Force. Anakin was close to his mother and loved her dearly, and he was utterly devastated when his mother perished in the hands of Tusken Raiders in their home planet of Tattoine. This started a chain of events that ultimately led Anakin to become angry, power-hungry and gullible to fall into the Dark Side. He later became the fearsome Sith Lord, Darth Vader.

5. Senator Palpatine / Darth Sidious (Born 83 BBY – Died 4 ABY. Was revived as a clone and born again in 10 ABY, died again in 11 ABY)

Senator Palpatine was the last Supreme Chancellor of the Galactic Empire and the First Emperor of the Galactic Empire. A Sith Lord that was considered as the strongest among his class throughout history, Palpatine's ultimate life goal was to overthrow the Jedi and the Republic and bring back the Sith Empire to power. He masterminded the construction of the Death Star and used his political power to destroy his ultimate enemies, the Jedis' from within. He turned Anakin's hate into a burning fuel that ultimately led Anakin to the Dark Side, after which he turned Anakin into his own apprentice and called him Darth Vader.

6. C3PO (Originally created 112 BBY – Rebuilt by Anakin around 32 BBY. Temporarily dismantled on 3 ABY)

Originally created in the planet of Affa in 112 BBY, C3PO was a protocol droid who possessed distinguished and unique characteristics that made him stand out from other droids. He was rebuilt by the young slave named Anakin Skywalker after he was gutted and thrown into the planet Tattoine. Throughout the history of the Star Wars universe, C3PO played vital roles in some of the most important and pivotal moments along with his counterpart, the astromechanical droid R2-D2. Although originally a droid programmed for etiquette and diplomatic relations, C3PO also served Anakin and his mother Shmi by performing household chores.

7. R2-D2 (Created 33 BBY – Destroyed 22 BBY, but was rebuilt shortly after)

An astromechanical droid who served under the Royal Engineers of Naboo aboard the starship of Queen Amidala, R2-D2 is a resourceful droid that fulfills various mechanical needs. From repairing starships to stopping elevators and projecting holograms, R2-D2 served a myriad of purpose to his masters and played a large role in the vital moments of galactic history. Brave and cunning, R2-D2 is always willing to use his tools and gadgets to help his master. Queen Amidala gave R2-D2 to Anakin Skywalker after he became a Jedi Knight. R2-D2 served Anakin faithfully throughout their time together by doing brave acts such as fighting alongside him or piloting and running his starship.

8. Shmi Skywalker (Born 72 BBY – Died 22 BBY)

As the oldest known ancestor of the Skywalker family, Shmi is one of the most enigmatic characters in Star Wars universe. The mother of the most powerful Jedi to ever wield the Force, Anakin Skywalker, he played a vital role in raising and taking care of his son. Shmi was born into slavery at a very early age and the whereabouts of the planet where she came from is still unknown. She conceived Anakin without a father, which was a huge mystery. It was believed that the midi-chlorians, the units of life that are responsible for a being's sensitivity to the Force, conceived Anakin themselves --- which explains why Anakin has such as high midi-chlorian count and why Shmi became pregnant even without a husband. Shmi was killed by the Tuskan Raiders in 22 BBY, which led to Anakin ultimately killing the whole tribe of Tuskan Raiders in anger and vengeance.

9. Master Yoda (Born 896 BBY – Died 4 ABY)

A legendary Jedi who was considered as one of the most powerful Jedis in the history of the Galaxy, Master Yoda served as a member of the Jedi Council for centuries. Small in stature and having an appearance that can easily deceive his enemies, Yoda possessed exceptional abilities in handling the light saber as well as controlling the Force. Yoda can manipulate and move objects without touching them and he can even hurl big blocks of metal and stone towards his enemies. He was the Master of the Order of the Jedi and trained almost every renowned Jedi in history, from Obi-Wan Kenobi to young Luke Skywalker. After the purging of the Jedi, which was masterminded by Palpatin, Yoda went into hiding and exiled himself in the faraway planet of Dagobah.

10. Mace Windu (Born 72 BBY – Died 19 BBY)

Serving as one of the highest leaders in the Jedi Order, alongside Yoda, Windu is a renowned Jedi Master and one of the last Jedi Masters to serve the Order before the purging was masterminded by Senator Palpatine. One of the best swordsman and wielders of the Force, Mace Windu was widely respected by his peers and feared by his enemies. He also created and mastered the Vaapad, the modern seventh generation of the light saber, which he used primarily as his combat weapon. He fought Palpatine in a duel after learning that Palpatine is a Sith Lord, but he was betrayed by Anakin Skywalker who was led to deception. He was subsequently killed by Palpatine after the Senator turned into Darth Sidious, falling to his death from Palpatine's window after being shocked by the Sith Lord's Force Lightning

Attack Of The Clones

*Note: The Galactic Standard Calendar was the standard measurement of time in the Star Wars Universe, centering the Coruscan solar cycle, which has 368 days --- with each day lasting 24 standard hours. The Battle of Yavin is used as a standard measuring point, with **BBY** standing for Before Battle of Yavin and **ABY** standing for After Battle of Yavin.*

1. Jango Fett (Born 66 BBY – Died 22 BBY)

A renowned and skillful Mandalorian bounty hunter, Jango was the definition of "assassin". He has established a reputation of being one of the strongest bounty hunters in the Galaxy and he became a seasoned veteran in taking jobs that many deemed impossible. Because of his prowess and skills, he was used as the genetic template for the clone army that the Republic built --- thus, leaving a legacy even after his death in the hands of Master Windu.

2. Boba Fett (Born 32 BBY – Died N/A)

Son of the man considered as one of the strongest, if not the strongest, bounty hunters in the history of the galaxy, Boba Fett was a genetic clone that was similar to his father Jango Fett. Even at a young age, Boba already shows prowess and skill in the ways of combat that no other kid in his age can compare to. After watching his father's head get decapitated by Master Windu, he started to harbor a strong feeling of hatred for the Jedi.

3. Bail Prestior Organa (Born 67 BBY – Died 0 BBY)

A friend of Jedi Masters such as Obi Wan Kenobi and Yoda, Bail Prestor Organa was a respected person who fought against the oppression of the Sith Empire. Upon the death of Queen Padme and the fall of Anakin to the Dark Side, Bail Organa adopted Padme's daughter, Leia. He was one of the most courageous fighters of the Republic. He died when the Death Star obliterated and destroyed his home planet Alderaan.

4. Mas Amedda

As one of Palpatine's trusted personnel and confidante, Mas Amedda served as the Vice Chairman of the Galactic Senate and continued to hold the position even after Palpatine turned the Republic into the Galactic Empire. Although it was known that Palpatine hated alien races, holding the second highest position in the Empire's political hierarchy meant that Mas Amedda was highly regarded by Palpatine, serving as his second-in-command and the political master when Palpatin isn't around.

5. Luminara Unduli (Born 58 BBY – Died 19 BBY)

During the final Years of the Galactic Republic before the usurpation of power by the Sith Lord Senatore Palpatine, Luminara Unduli served as one of the most capable female Jedi Knights. She was a formidable Jedi who fought in renowned battles. At a young age, she was detected to be Force-sensitive and taken under the wing of the Jedi Order, which allowed her to escape the horrors of his planet Miral --- a cold and dry planet that was severely oppressed by the Trade Federation. She died in the Battle of Kashyyyk.

6. Queen Jamillia

Queen Jamillia is an enigmatic figure who served as the successor of Queen Amidala as the elected sovereign of planet Naboo. She also convinced Amidala to run as a Senator, trusting that her good heart would bring peace, justice and prosperity to the Galaxy. During the Separatist Crisis, Queen Jamilia opened Naboo to aid the refugees who were fleeing from the hands of the Empire after the Galactic Republic was abolished. This caused a lot of criticism from unions who did not want to wrath of the Empire unleashed onto them such as the Spice Miners of Naboo.

7. Captain Gregor Typho (Born N/A – Died 19 BBY)

Serving as the head of the security for Queen Padme Amidala during the Separatist Crisis and the Clone Wars, Gregor Typho was quiet but skilled in battle. As a junior guard during the Battle of Naboo in 32 BBY, Gregor Typho fought with distinction and was thus elevated into a higher position. This battle left him with many scars, including the loss of his left eye, but did not hinder him from protecting the Queen. He was always seen accompanying Queen Padme during her diplomatic missions.

8. Kit Fisto (Born N/A – Died 19 BBY)

One of the most renowned Nautolan and one of the first to become a Jedi Master, Kit Fisto was one of the last Jedis to fight in the waning years of the Galactic Republic. He had large eyes and a tangle of tentacles extending from his head, typical of a Nautolan alien race. Known for his friendly gesture and smile, Kit Fisto died alongside Master Windu during the duel in Palpatine's office where Palpatine was discovered by Mace Mindu to be a Dark Sith Lord in disguise.

9. Ki-Adi-Mundi (Born 92 BBY – Died 19 BBY)

Ki-Adi-Mundi was a Cerean male Jedi Master who served the High Jedi Council during the waning years of the Galactic Republic. Even at a very young age, Ki-Adi-Mundi was discovered to be highly sensitive and he started training at 4 years old. Although Jedis have a rule banning them from having wives and bearing children, Ki-Adi-Mundi was exempted from this rule due to the fact that his species has a very low birth rate. He had 5 wives and seven children that he left while he was out doing missions for the Jedi Order. He was shot to death by the Republic's own Storm Trooper during the Great Jedi Purge.

10. Saesee Tiin (Born N/A – Died 19 BBY)

A skilled master of the arts of wielding the light saber and piloting star fighters, Saesee Tiin was one of the last Jedi Masters to serve the Jedi Council during the last few years of the Galactic Republic. He was a member of the Iktotchi race, and he has an imposing physical characteristic, standing tall and having two horns protruding from his ears.

11. Plo Koon (Born N/A – Died 19 BBY)

As one of the calmest and wisest members of the Jedi Council, Plo Koon commanded a high level of respect even among his contemporaries in the high Jedi Council. His analysis of events and his way of devising plans to counteract enemy attacks are some of his very important traits, and his wisdom was even compared to that of Master Yoda. He was also a very strong combatant who became a Jedi General, fighting in known conflicts such as the Battle of Felucia and Battle of Abregado. Just like the other members of the Jedi Council, he was executed by his own Storm Troopers when Order 66 was executed.

12. Count Dooku (Born 102 BBY – Died 19 BBY)

Once a Jedi Master who was Padawan to the great Yoda himself, Dooku fell to the Dark Side of the Force because of his disagreements with the Jedi High Council. His sensitivity to the Force was great and he was taken to train under the ways of the Jedi at a very early age. He even trained the great Qui-Gon Jinn as his Padawan when he became a Jedi Knight, which shows his high level of skill and sensitivity to the Force. Upon the orders of his own Sith Lord, Senator Palpatine, Count Dooku was killed and executed by the Jedi Knight Anakin Skywalker, who would soon fall under the same path of falling into the Dark Side.

13. Sly Moore

Although serving as a Force-sensitive female Umbaran in the Galactic Republic, Sly Moore was secretly under the service and command of the Dark Sith Lord Sidious, also known as Senator Palpatine. She developed a strong bond and loyalty to the Dark Lord Sidious, who uncharacteristically showed care for her and adopted her after she was kidnapped by Darth Maul and trapped for months in an ancient tomb where dead Sith Lords tortured her mentally and spiritually. She was one of the closest confidants and aides of Lord Sidious who posed as Senator Palpatine during their political travels.

14. Barriss Offee (Born 40 BBY – Died 19 BBY)

Known as a very talented and well-known Jedi Healer during the last years of the Galactic Republic, Barriss Offee ascended into knighthood during the battle known as the Clone Wars. She helped Obi-Wan Kenobi and young Anakin Skywalker settle a border dispute on the planet Ansion, which resulted to her gaining respect from the two Jedi Knights. She was killed during the execution of Order 66 in an event known as the Great Jedi Purge.

Revenge Of The Sith

Note: The Galactic Standard Calendar was the standard measurement of time in the Star Wars Universe, centering the Coruscan solar cycle, which has 368 days --- with each day lasting 24 standard hours. The Battle of Yavin is used as a standard measuring point, with BBY standing for Before Battle of Yavin and ABY standing for After Battle of Yavin.

1. Tarrful

A male chieftain from the Wookie clan who fought alongside Yoda during the Purging of the Jedi in Year 19 BBY, Tarrful was a long-time friend of Chewbacca. He had good relations with the Jedi Masters and he even fought during the Battle of Kashyyyk. He had significant contributions in the war such as planning of attack points and important placements of soldiers, which led to many significant victories for the Republic.

2. San Hill (Born N/A - Died 19 BBY)

As the chairman of the Intergalactic Bank, San Hill held significant power not only financially but also politically. By building connections with people and networking with the powers-that-be, San Hill placed himself in position to profit from the wars fought between the Empire and the Republic. By pledging his support to the cause of the Separatists and by backing the Confederacy of Independent Systems, he caught the irk of the Empire. He was killed by Darth Vader during the end of the Clone Wars.

3. Pooja Naberrie

Daughter of one of the ruling elite families from the Planet of Naboo, Pooja was one of the members from the families who attended the funeral of Queen Padmé Amidala. Pooja's family supported most, if not all, of the endeavors of the late Queen Padmé who was well-loved by her own people.

4. Wilhuff Tarkin (Born 64 BBY - Died 0 BBY or during Battle of Yavin)

A male Human who held one of the highest positions in the Galactic Empire, Wilhuff Tarkin was one of the driving forces behind the Imperial Doctrine and he contributed greatly to the creation of the Death Star. Born from the powerful and militaristic family of the Tarkin Clan, Wilhuff gained a lot of popularity due to his war conquests and tales of battles that he commanded to victory. He was a vocal supported of the Sith Lord, Senator Palpatine also known as Darth Sidious.

5. Chewbacca (Born 200 BBY - Died N/A)

Also known as "Chewie" among his close comrades, Chewbacca was a Wookie male warrior that was known for "hooking up with the wrong people", although not with bad intentions. He was a co-pilot of the smuggler Hans Solo in the starship Millenium Falcon. Although not really evident because of his playful nature, Chewie is a great warrior who fought with Yoda and the Jedi during the Clone Wars and served as a hero of the group called The Alliance To Restore The Republic

6. Beru Whitesun Lars (Born 47 BBY - Died 0 BBY)

The wife of Owen Lars, the stepbrother of Anakin Skywalker, Beru Whitesun Lars was the woman who raised Luke Skywalker as if he was her own. Living most of her life as a moisture farmer, she guided Luke Skywalker into a path of normal life --- knowing all too well the history of the Skywalkers. Luke's father, her brother-in-law Anakin Skywalker, fell to the Dark Side of the Force after being devoured by anger and sadness --- something that Beru has tried to avoid happening to Luke. Beru was a sweet and kind lady, which could be the reason to Luke's soft demeanor at times.

7. Owen Lars (52 BBY - Died 0 BBY)

Owen Lars was the son of Cliegg Lars, the man who freed Anakin's mother (also his own mother) from slavery and married her. Just like his father, Owen had a no-nonsense demeanor and would always ask Luke to "help out in the farm" in order to sway him away from discovering his true nature --- that of a Force-sensitive human. He and his wife Beru died after the Imperial Stormtroopers went after Luke Skywalker and he spat on the face of the troopers' commanding officer.

8. Droideka

Droidekas are also known as Destroyer Droids or Rolling Droids. These are war droids that were used by the Trade Federation during the battles at the Invasion of Naboo and were known as "rolling droids" because of how they move their bodies around. They transform their shapes by rolling into balls and this maneuver allows them to move up to 75 kilometers per hour.

9. Plo Koon (Born N/A - Died 19 BBY)

A Kel dor Jedi Master who once served as a member of the high Jedi Council during the waning years of the Galactic Republic, Plo Koon was skilled not only in the ways of the Force but also with the sword. He became a Jedi General and rose to ranks during the Clone Wars, leading his own troops of starfighters as one of the most competent pilots that the Republic had in service. He was also a good friend if Qui-Gon Jinn, but he refused training young Anakin Skywalker due to the boy's young age. During the end of the Clone Wars, he was executed by his own forces under the Order No. 66.

10. 2-1B

2-1B was a medical droid who treated the fallen Darth Vader after he lost his battle against his former Jedi Master, Obi-Wan Kenobi. After suffering from the burn and the amputation of his legs, Darth Vader was almost killed by the flowing lava and the loss of blood. 2-1B was one of the most advanced medical droids during that time, who helped save Darth Vader's life.

11. Boga

Boga was a female Varactyl who had an iridescent green-pebbled skin that shines with a blue color. About 4-meters tall at her shoulders, Boga possessed very strong limbs with curled claws that allowed her to not only run fast but run along walls too. During his stay at the planet Utapau, Obi-Wan Kenobi took a liking to Boga and used her as a riding companion.

12. Tion Medon

The leader of the planet Utapau and port administrator of the Pau City on Utapau, Tion Medon held great influence on the logistics and the transportation of goods and people around his domain. During the waning days of the Clone Wars, Tion Medon was coerced to help General Grievous and his associates by bringing them in a sanctuary. After Grievous threatened to destroy Medon's city if he did not assist, Tion Meddon was forced to agree. Still, Grievous was hunted and tracked by Jedi Master Obi-Wan Kenobi, and Tion Medon assisted in bringing Grievous down.

13. Ask Aak

As one of the closest confidantes and part of Senator Palpatine's inner circle, Ask Aak held great power both in political and military factions. He targeted the Confederacy of Independent Systems to stop people from rebelling against the Galactic Empire. He was also in on the secret of Order No. 66 which ultimately led to the execution of numerous Jedi and Republic forces.

14. Raymus Antilles (born N/A - Died 0 BBY)

A human male who came from the peaceful, prominent and powerful planet of Alderaan, Raymus Antilles was educated in diplomacy and learned the art of piloting a starship even at a young age. Shortly before the Battle of Yavin, Raymus Antilles met with the forces of the Empire while trying to help Princess Leia escape. During this encounter, he was killed by Darth Vader who proved too powerful for him and he died protecting Princess Leia.

15. R4-P17

As one of the astromech droid partners of Obi-Wan Kenobi, R4-P17 was present in almost every important moment during the stretch of the Clone Wars. But, because of the exposure to the Jedi Master's frequent battles, he was also destroyed by Buzz Droids during the Battle of Coruscant.

RETURN OF THE

JEDI

Note: The Galactic Standard Calendar was the standard measurement of time in the Star Wars Universe, centering the Coruscan solar cycle, which has 368 days --- with each day lasting 24 standard hours. The Battle of Yavin is used as a standard measuring point, with BBY standing for Before Battle of Yavin and ABY standing for After Battle of Yavin.

1. 8B8

Originally a smelter droid that was manufactured by Verpine Roche Hive, 8D8 was programmed to do simple tasks in mining and ore-extraction facilities. That is, until he came into the possession of Jabba the Hutt, who reprogrammed him to torture other droids. He often terrorized the other droids and threatened to smelt them if they do not keep in line. He also resented the more sophisticated protocol and astromech droids.

2. Gial Ackbar (Born 41 BBY - Died 29 ABY)

The primary military commander of the Alliance To Restore The Republic and its successor, the New Republic, Gial Ackbar was a military genius who led the Rebel Alliance to a myriad of victories against the Empire. After a long and fruitful service to the Republic, Ackbar retired to a quiet life, content with his writing and his memoirs. At 29 ABY, we died of old age.

3. Aldar Beedo

Aldar Beedo was a skilled podracer from Ploo-II who once competed in the Boonta Eve Classic on the planet Tatooine against Anakin Skywalker. Unlike several of the other competitors who had their pods destroyed while racing, Aldar Beedo was able to complete the whole race and even finished in third place behind Xexto Gasgano and the Force-sensitive human Anakin Skywalker.

4. Amanaman

A mysterious Amani bounty hunter who appeared in "Return of the Jedi", Amani prefers the use of traditional hunting weapons instead of firing away with the laser blasters. He keeps the skulls of his victims tied onto his staff as a token of victory and memento.

5. Barada (Born N/A - Died 4 ABY)

Chief engineer of Jabba's Sail Barge. Serving as a crime underling and minion to the underground gang boss Jabba The Hutt, Barada was imprisoned along with Luke Skywalker and Leia Organa when Jabba attempted to execute a group of Rebels in the Great Pit of Carkoon. During the commotion, when prisoners tried to fight to free themselves, Luke Skywalker slashed Barada with his lightsaber, effectively killing Barada in the process.

6. Bib Fortuna (Born N/A - Died 4 ABY)

Bib fortuna was a male Twi'lek who served as the right hand man to Jabba the Hutt and provided irreplaceable service in Jabba's crime syndicate. As Jabba's right hand, majordomo and chief of staff for decades, he oversees all of the day-to-day operations and serves in his master's place when Jabba the Hutt isn't around. During the Boonta Eve Classic on Tattoine, he was also able to witness the young Anakin Skywalker win the first place in pod racing. He died during the commotion that occurred when Han Solo was rescued by his comrades, led by Luke Skywalker.

7. Boushh (Born N/A - Died 4 ABY)

Known as a bounty hunter cunning and deceitful enough to blackmail even his own clients, Boushh was best known as the Bounty Hunter that Princess Leia disguised herself as in order to penetrate and infiltrate Jabba's palace in the hopes of rescuing Han Solo.

8. Buboicullaar

Buboicullaar, also called Bubo by Jabba, was a male frog-dog that was kept as a pet by Jabba the Hutt. Silent and often looking very dumb, Bubo is actually surprisingly smarter than most of Jabba's minions and thugs. At first glance, he seems to be clueless and stupid, but he is more than just a guard animal for Jabba the Hutt.

9. Crix Madine (Born 31 BBY - Died 12 ABY)

As a general who served for the Rebel Alliance (which later became the New Republic after the Empire was overthrown), Crix Madine was the officer responsible for planning stealthy tactics and covert missions. Unknown to some, Crix was the one who devised the attack on the Endor shield generator. He also mentored and trained the soldiers who accompanied the smuggler Han Solo to a mission on the forest moon.

10. Klaatu (Born N/A - Died 4 ABY)

Klaatu was a green Nikto gambler who employed by the underground crime lord and syndicate head Jabba the Hutt. If he was not repairing his lord Jabba's boats, Klaatu spent time enjoying all the executions that Jabba initiates inside his palace. During the failed execution of Luke Skywalker and his companions, Klaatu was killed while aboard his master's sail barge.

Made in the USA
San Bernardino, CA
08 December 2016